MAKE ROJAVA GREEN AGAIN

Building an ecological society

INTERNATIONALIST
COMMUNE OF ROJAVA

Illustrated by
MATT BONNER

INTERNATIONALIST
COMMUNE OF ROJAVA

IN COOPERATION WITH THE
DEMOCRATIC SELF-GOVERNANCE
OF NORTHERN SYRIA

First published in London, 2018 by Dog Section Press
and Internationalist Commune of Rojava
Printed by Calverts Ltd., a workers' cooperative

ISBN 9780993543562

Graphic design by Matt Bonner - revoltdesign.org
Dog Section Press logo by Marco Bevilacqua

CONTENTS

KURDISTAN

TURKEY

KOBANI

TELL ABYAD

AFRIN

ALEPPO

SYRIA

ROJAVA

Democratic Federation
of Northern Syria

DÊRIKA HEMKO

QAMISHLO

SERÊ KANÎYÊ

ROJAVA

AL-HASAKAH

IRAQ

QQA

DEDICATION

The freedom to face the challenges of building an ecological society in Northern Syria is, first and foremost, due to the many martyrs of this revolution. Without their struggle, there would be no liberated ground in Rojava on which to sow the seeds of ecological living. This book is dedicated to them.

> "
>
> Help bring a new world
> into being in Rojava. And
> spread its vision: that a
> free, ecological society is
> possible everywhere.
>
> "

DEBBIE BOOKCHIN

FOREWORD

by Debbie Bookchin

I t is impossible to ignore the fact that this beautiful book was first published in late 2018, in the shadow of Turkey's invasion of the largely-Kurdish canton of Afrîn in northern Syria. As the heroic fighters of the YPG and all-female YPJ continue to fight off the fascist thugs mobilised by Turkey wishing to impose its authoritarian, anti-woman, ecologically-rapacious, capitalist ideology on Afrîn (and, if Turkey had its way, on Cizîrê and Kobanî, the other two cantons of Rojava, more formally known as the Democratic Federation of Northern Syria) outside observers often ask: "What is it about the social structures of Rojava that so inspires the fierce loyalty of its defenders and its people?"

This book answers that question. In language that bridges the utopian and the concrete, the poetic and the everyday, the Internationalist Commune of Rojava has produced both a vision and a manual for what a free, ecological society can look like. In these pages you will find a philosophical introduction to the idea of social ecology, a theory that argues that only when we end the hierarchical relations between human beings (men over women, old over young, one ethnicity or religion over another, and other forms of domination) will we be able to heal our relationship with the natural world. As the writers observe, the imperative for this healing grows stronger every day as global warming and neoliberal ideology threaten the very viability of human life on this planet.

In keeping with the Internationalist Commune's implicit recognition that theory is useless unless put into practice, you will also find in this book a concrete guide to the building of an ecological community in this corner of the world, a region that has been torn by war, its natural wonders and resources so abused by tyrants of the past. As you read this book, you will be enthralled by the descriptions of the rivers and lakes, the sweeping steppes flowing with wheat and cotton, lentils, chickpeas and beans, the farmland and the fruit trees – apricot, pomegranate, fig, cherry, and so many others, that they are planting to help make Rojava green again. Indeed, in 2018 alone, they are going to seed 10,000 saplings that will someday be used to support local air quality and the continued reforestation of the Hayaka Nature Reserve near Dêrîk in the canton of Cizîrê, an important wildlife area where wolves, foxes, wild pigs, and all sorts of birds have found refuge, and where people can experience the beauty and solitude of woodlands. This project is deeply moving in its commitment to the long-term ecological health of the region. It speaks to our profound need as human beings to steward nature's rich abundance. It offers living proof that with a thoughtful democratic process in place, an egalitarian and ecological society is feasible – a better world is possible.

The authors astutely observe that an ecological society must have the economic and political foundation to support it: a communalist, or democratic confederalist, model in which every member of society has a voice and investment in its future well-being. In such a world, where people together decide how to use natural resources, we can rethink relationships between urban and rural life, production and consumption, the periphery and the core, and chart a rational use of land and water, of renewable energy resources, and even of waste. This book offers ideas, and examples of ways that the unique landscape of Rojava can support its people. And in doing so – in the presentation of both theory and elegant practical solutions – the Internationalist Commune provides inspiration for building an ecological society not only in Rojava, but everywhere.

The Internationalist Commune comprises a group of people from all corners of the world who have come to Rojava to lend their support and expertise, their ideas, and, most importantly (and quite literally), their hands. They want to build a society that promotes a healthy and harmonious future for the people of this region and the natural resources on which they depend. Thrillingly, they invite you to join them: in building the Academy that will serve to introduce foreigners to life in Rojava, and in sustaining the projects they have already begun. I expect that, like me, you will be impelled by the sense of hope, possibility, and utopian vision that Rojava represents to the Middle East and rest of the world. Share this vision with friends, lend your expertise, and support Rojava's Internationalist Commune. Help bring a new world into being in Rojava. And spread its vision: that a free, ecological society is possible everywhere.

INTRODUCTION

Although the environmental challenges in Rojava caught our attention from the beginning, the development of our community's ecological work has been a slow process. The starting point was that for internationalists in Rojava it was an important experience to participate in the revolution not only with our minds, but also with our hands. And what could be better than working with the very ground on which this revolution is taking place? Thinking about what we could do for the revolution, we came up with the idea of setting up a tree nursery in the Internationalist Academy.

Questions arose with the construction of our Academy and the plan for the tree nursery, which led to more questions. Where does the water that we need for the Academy, as well as the trees, come from? What happens to our waste-water? What do we do with our garbage, and what does society do with it? Which nutrients do we need for our vegetable garden and which are used in the surrounding agriculture? Why is only wheat grown around the Academy today, where forests still stood just a few decades ago? The more we asked, discussed and worked, the clearer we became about the connection between the ecological problem and the economic and political situation. It was this process that led us to ask: what would an ecological society in Rojava look like, and how could it be built?

It seemed appropriate for us to share our preliminary discussions and research results, and this is what we want to do with this book. It is meant not only for those involved with the relevant committees and all the other people who work and research locally, but also for activists, scientists and interested people all over the world. Environmental issues in Rojava have been a subject of little concern, both within local structures and in global solidarity circles. The general public abroad has ignored this issue so far, as the coverage of the war against the Islamic State continues to drown out the political nature of this revolution. With this short book we want to suggest a different emphasis: to report on the urgent challenges for people and nature in Rojava; highlight the ecological work here; and engage in an active dialogue with all those interested and in a position to help.

This also presented us with a challenge when writing this book: how do we combine ideological discussions about the fundamental relationship between people and nature with research on questions of biology and building construction? How do we manage to make these topics accessible and not just for people who are already familiar with them? We hope that this has been achieved by the breadth of the topics addressed, the diversity of the texts, and their division into usable sections.

To begin, we introduce ourselves, the Internationalist Commune of Rojava. In the following chapter we will introduce our discussion of social ecology and our outlook on an ecological society, which is the theoretical basis of our ongoing work. Since we can't take knowledge of the impact of capitalist modernity on the ecological system for granted, a theoretical introduction to the ecological crisis of capitalist modernity follows. We have tried to take into account the many different aspects of this crisis.

Based on this global perspective of the ecological crisis, in the fifth chapter we will discuss the situation in Rojava, with particular reference to the largest canton in Rojava, Cizîrê. On the one hand, this focus is due to the central importance of Cizîrê for energy, environmental and agricultural policy issues, and on the other hand on the fact that we are working and building our Academy here. It has not been possible, as of this publication date, to travel to the canton of Afrîn, so we were only able to conduct limited research on the situation there; Chapter 5 also gives an overview of ecological issues in the context of the policies of the Turkish and Syrian states.

We will formulate in detail our proposals as to what further steps can be taken in the construction of an ecological society. The detailed information, facts and figures we refer to in this chapter are based on studies listed in the bibliography at the end of the book and on detailed discussions with those in charge of the various structures of the democratic self-administration. By this we mean the democratic non-state structures, based on neighborhood councils, which have been built up since the beginning of the revolution in 2011.

Taking into account this information, the analysis of the situation, and the projects undertaken so far, we have determined the objectives of the "Make Rojava Green Again" campaign and the next concrete steps in it. We will present these in detail at the end of the book.

The Internationalist Commune of Rojava
September 2018

INTRODUCTION

"

Above all be sensitive,
in the deepest areas
of yourselves, to any
injustice committed
against whoever it may
be anywhere in the
world. This is the most
beautiful characteristic of
a revolutionary.

"

CHE GUEVARA

INTERNATIONALIST COMMUNE OF ROJAVA

Learn. Support. Organise.

Six years have passed since the beginning of the revolution in Rojava. Since the heroic resistance of Kobanî, the YPJ/YPG continue to push back the reactionary gangs of ISIS. At the same time, the people of Rojava successfully resist all attempts to corrupt the revolution. Inspired and informed by the ideas of Abdullah Öcalan and the struggle of the Kurdish liberation movement, built on women's liberation, ecology and radical democracy, a revolutionary movement is organising itself in Rojava to bring an end to capitalist modernity. But the revolution in Rojava is under pressure: the war against ISIS, the daily terror of the Turkish state, as well as a broad economic embargo, are slowing down the construction of the new society. In this situation, Rojava needs worldwide support more than ever.

Rojava requires media attention and political support from outside; at the same time the people in Rojava need localised, concrete help. Doctors and English teachers, translators and engineers: the institutions and structures in Rojava need knowledge and ideas. But it is not only about experts. We are looking for people who want to learn, participate and become a part of the revolution. Internationalism and direct action – whether in YPJ and YPG or in civil structures – helps to express the meaning of the revolution, and spreads it beyond Kurdistan and the Middle East. Alongside practical solidarity, it is urgently needed.

> **"**
>
> ## You are the hope by yourselves.
>
> **"**

ABDULLAH ÖCALAN

Rojava needs us, but even more we need Rojava. We need hope, faith, inspiration, and new perspectives in a collective struggle against oppression.

In the Western world the authoritarian state and right-wing movements are celebrating their comeback – the former stars of neoliberalism are already on their way to open fascism. Trump, Erdogan, and Putin are removing the last masks of democracy. In the face of these developments, most revolutionary movements stand frozen. Marginalised and without perspective, scattered and estranged, the only role the system leaves for them is to observe and to criticise.

Rojava presents a way to overcome this dilemma: Learning from the Kurdish movement means to organise and spread the revolution.

> **"**
>
> # Create two, three, many Rojavas!
>
> **"**

Although internationalists have already been working in Rojava for many years, up until now there has been no established system to bring many people from abroad to Rojava and to integrate them into the structures of the revolution. In addition to the logistical problems of travelling to Rojava, the absence of language skills, cultural differences, and a lack of knowledge of the movement as well as the region, have prevented the meaningful participation of internationalists in revolutionary work. Local structures to educate and prepare internationalists, and support local institutions in their work and interaction with internationalists, are missing. Simply put, a system to organise internationalist work in Rojava is needed.

We are building up this self-organised and self-funded system together with the Kurdish liberation movement. The first step will be to establish an Academy for internationalists in Rojava. There we will organise political-cultural education, language courses and collective, practical work. This will enable internationalists to participate in the local structures.

We call on everyone to organise themselves in order to support the revolution in Rojava, and to follow and engage in the activities of the Internationalist Commune.

In a neighborhood in Qamishlo, a mother greets the anniversary of the revolution in Rojava.

SOCIAL ECOLOGY

A look at humanity and nature

The world of the 21st century faces the ruins of its past and present. War has become a normal state, poverty and hunger marginal news that no longer merit headlines. Many people have lost the meaning and significance of being human, and the word society means only isolated individuals subsumed under a state that manages their interpersonal relationships. Given these developments, environmental issues seem to be secondary – incidental to many, something for environmentalists to worry about.

But the ecological crisis has become the most urgent challenge of our time, because it touches and impacts all areas of society. The ecosystem has been wrecked to such an extent that much of the damage has become irreversible. A large part of life, both human and natural, has entered a stage of crisis. On this note, Abdullah Öcalan writes: "A policy that promises salvation from the present crisis can only lead to a proper social system if it is ecological."

It is necessary to outline such an ecological social system and to develop a policy that can overcome the ecological and social crisis as a whole: a policy that not only fights the symptoms, but that recognises that the ecological crisis and the societal crisis are intimately linked. In order to solve the ecological crisis, we must change the social relations of power and domination fundamentally.

If we take this as our starting point in the search for new ways to live, we must also be able to answer the question of how and why societies have ended up in opposition to nature. From a historical perspective, we must be able to identify the decisive moments of social change that led to the break between nature and society that we see today in capitalist society. To speak simply of humanity and not of concrete mentalities, systems, and rulers, only hides the causes and leads us to false premises. It conceals the contradictions that lie behind the categories of humanity: the antagonisms between oppressed and oppressors; men and women; old and young; light and dark; and the rich and the poor.

To be successful in building a new social-ecological society we have to conceive of the human being as a life form that, with its creativity and creative power, can make a great contribution to the improvement of the entire natural world. Even more than that, it is our obligation to accept this potential in ourselves, and to believe in it. It's clear that solving the ecological crisis, and moving towards a social-ecological society, cannot be left to science and technology alone: it is also the task of a critical theory that is able to overcome the division between humanity and nature.

Many thinkers – Abdullah Öcalan, Silvia Federici, Friedrich Engels, and Murray Bookchin, in particular –

have played an important role in contributing to such a theory, with their analyses of social power relations and historical developments, their understanding of nature and humanity, and their firm belief in the viability of an ecological, free society.

THE HISTORICAL CHANGES IN THE RELATIONSHIP BETWEEN SOCIETY AND NATURE

When we look at the changes in society's relationship to nature, it is vital not to lose sight of the changes in societal power-relations, modes of production, and ideology. There is not a single societal relationship with nature: different modes of production, social classes, cultures and genders develop different relations. Nature includes various aspects, like food and energy, but also an individual's relationship with her or his body. It's about how the external world around the human is seen, understood and felt.

The current relationship with nature, dominated by the state-capitalist structure of society, developed from a long process of change. To disconnect this relationship from its development gives it the appearance of a system that has always been inevitable. Failure to analyse this history and its development results in an inability to understand the present or construct the future. With this in mind, in the following section we will look at some aspects of the changes in society's relationship with nature.

> **❝**
>
> The human: nature become self-aware.
>
> **❞**

JOHANN GOTTLIEB FICHTE

Natural society can be understood as the first social form. In small communities of clans, human beings began the process of becoming socialised.

In early societies people's understanding of nature was characterised by a close connection with it; nature was regarded as something living, embracing the idea that every natural entity had a soul. The experience of nature found its expression in the idea of spirits, with which humanity sought an understanding. Humans had to live in harmony with these forces, because they determined life and its rhythms. People didn't try to conquer nature, but to influence it through magical rituals, to appeal to the spirits of nature. This magic was based on the observations of the processes of life and death in nature and human beings themselves. The life of humans, in small clan communities and with an idea of living nature, ran according to the basic principles of ecology – that is, in harmony with nature and each other.

So we can define the natural society as "a spontaneous form of an ecological society" (Öcalan). In the collective memory of humanity, nature is like a mother, giving people life and its necessities. The term 'mother nature' can be traced back to this collective experience.

THE RULE OF MAN OVER HUMANITY AND NATURE

The life of the first communities was based on what people could gather from nature, but hunting came to augment the collecting of plants and fruits. The systematic and deliberate killing of animals evolved into a hunting culture. Out of this, and the emerging conflicts between clan communities, a culture of war developed that went beyond self-defence. The foundation was laid for the further development of a war mentality and its associated institutions and hierarchies, and this had serious consequences for the development of society. In parallel with the arrival of the first hierarchies and the division of people into categories and classes (such as race and gender), the relationship with nature also changed.

By observing the natural processes of birth, growth and death, we developed the first understanding of biology that led to the deliberate use of plants and livestock in agriculture. Humans began to shape the environment according to their needs, and to influence the biological development of animals and plants. Increasing yields from agriculture that went beyond the level of immediate needs now had to be managed.

This administration of social wealth was closely connected with the emergence of social hierarchy (which had already

found its expression in the dominion of the old over young, men over women, and leaders over the led). In the course of this process, these hierarchies were increasingly transformed into a more complex social system – as we see in the development of Sumerian and Egyptian priests. These first state structures were legitimised by a mythological system that eliminated the spirits of nature and placed gods – and their human interpreters – above them. And just as the new gods were enthroned above nature, their new priests ruled over society like gods.

From the perspective of the new mythology [...] nature and the universe are full of ruling, punishing gods. These gods actually oppressive and exploiting despots are located outside of nature [...]. It's like they dried out nature. It develops a view of an inanimate nature and matter. All living beings are humiliated, and servants created from the excrement of the gods.

ABDULLAH ÖCALAN

In this process, we find the interweaving of man's dominion over man with man's dominion over nature. Moving from a free and ecological co-existence in natural society, with mutual respect, solidarity and care, towards a society based on hierarchies, classes and domination, people alienated themselves not only from each other, but also from nature. This was the beginning of our downfall, because the evolving class society developed in clear contradiction to nature. The idea of a living, animated, colourful and productive nature gave way to one of a vindictive and mean-spirited nature – something to compete with. Beginning with Sumerian society, this counter-revolution against the natural society, accompanied by a radical change in the mentality of the people, gradually spread throughout the Middle East until it fundamentally changed large parts of the world.

The idea of nature as merciless, oppressive and dominating, which still persists today, goes back to this break in the social relationship. Humanity, confronted with this oppressive force as a small, naked and fragile creature, must protect itself and develop its own powers in order to conquer nature, to become its ruler. This understanding then served to justify the increasingly oppressive relations of people among themselves. According to this doctrine, humanity can escape the power of nature through the productivity of enslavement. Our collective survival depends on the power of human labour. At the same time, the suffering of the enslaved seems a small thing when compared with the acquired power of man over nature; the enslaved are the collateral damage of the liberation of mankind.

> **❝**
>
> The return to nature and the lived world,
> which had always been demonised.
>
> **❞**

ABDULLAH ÖCALAN

Society's relationship with nature was not fundamentally changed in Europe until the Reformation. The determination of people to break away from the Church's dogmas led to a return to rationality and the everyday, which had been demonised by Christianity. The idea of an animated, living nature, in which God Himself lived, found its place again in the imagination of the people. In art, this was expressed in the depiction of nature and people in realistic forms, showing their beauty. This ended the mentality that treated nature and the environment as something inert.

At the same time, the state tried further to dissolve the social knowledge system of natural healing – of birth, life and the human body. This knowledge came from millennia of women's experiences, who developed it and passed it on. Women who believed in the power of natural ways and had a deep relationship with nature were executed during the Inquisition. Possessing this knowledge was seen as the work of the devil and the women were called witches. They were considered remnants of the times in which myths, goddess cults and belief in nature existed along with the worship of natural places. The attack on women and the femicide committed against them also represented an attack on the social bond with nature and knowledge of it.

This attack wasn't limited to the societies in the global North: with colonialism, social relations of nature in the global South have increasingly been subjected to the paradigms of exploitation, destruction and centralisation of social knowledge. At the same time, the ideas of the indigenous populations of the colonies exerted a great fascination. Their attachment to nature and freedom, lack of institutionalised conditions of exploitation, and their participation in a collective community that left little room for individual greed, reminded people from war-torn Europe of the natural society.

The centralisation of agriculture, the expropriation of peasant land, and migration to cities further destroyed society's knowledge of ecological processes and its links to nature. The seizure of land by feudal lords converted large parts of previously collective land into the private possessions of individuals.

> **"**
>
> **In modern times humans have become a wolf not only to humans, but to all nature.**
>
> **"**

ABDULLAH ÖCALAN

With the development of science as a method for explaining the world, the understanding of natural biological processes also deepened and spread. This was defined more and more in a scientific way and described in rational rather than religious terms. Humanity detached itself from nature; it again put itself at the centre of things, and now considered nature and even the human body as inert and static objects for research. The transition from a holistic world view, which regarded nature as animated, to a mechanistic worldview of positivist ideology, was a decisive step in the change in the social relationship with nature. Nature became inanimate matter that could be worked, divided, measured, examined and controlled – a resource that might have a price, but no value as mere life.

Often, nature is understood as all-determining. The individual human being and society itself are reduced to zoological entities that follow the law of nature – the survival of the fittest. Competition and enmity projected onto nature are reflected in people and social affairs. War, violence, domination, and oppression are viewed as natural things from which there is no escape. This can only be controlled, if at all, by a supernatural and superhuman entity, the authoritarian state, as proposed by Hobbes. The difference between humanity and nature dissolves almost completely; it is only the ability to think that differentiates humans from animals. Here lies the possibility of individual reason and will and, with this, the instinctiveness of body and nature can be disciplined.

The bourgeois Enlightenment wanted to take away humanity's fear of nature, so that nature could be completely subjected to its own ends. The prerequisite for this was knowledge of physical laws and technical tools. Nature and society face each other in a dualistic, hostile relationship; it isn't surprising that such a relationship with nature elicited other reactions. An attitude developed that did not regard nature as the enemy of society, but society as the enemy of nature. In the face of increasingly frightening environmental catastrophes, for which humanity is responsible, there is resignation and pessimism regarding civilisation, society, and even humanity itself. Technology is shown in contrast to innocent, organic nature; science opposed to reverence for life; reason against innocent intuition; more or less, humanity against all of life. It's argued that humanity should, therefore, subordinate itself to nature and subject itself to nature's rules. But even in this primitivist understanding of nature and humanity, their inner opposition – their duality – persists.

The deep alienation between humanity and nature and between people and their bodies is the legacy of positivist science. It is the absolute object-subject relationship that has entered human thinking via positivism and determines the basis of the social relationship of nature in capitalist modernity. The development of this mentality, this conception of nature, became part of the process of increasingly centralised social systems, including the modern nation-state. This mentality is interwoven with industrialisation, the development of machinery and engines. The impact of this hierarchical, industrial economy on soil, air, water, and people has expanded to such an extent that the ecological system is now irreversibly damaged.

THE CAPITALIST MODERNITY:
PROFIT AND ENRICHMENT AS THE
MEANING OF THE EXISTENCE OF ALL LIFE

A person alienated from nature is alienated from and destroying his- or herself. No system has shown this connection more clearly than capitalist modernity; environmental destruction and ecological crises go hand in hand with the oppression and exploitation of people. Capitalist modernity, which makes a commodity of everything, has not even stopped at the limits of life itself: through new technologies (such as genetic engineering) life itself is commodified. In capitalist modernity, the system commands the entire planet, as it commands life itself.

Capitalism's spread to all areas of life seems to have no end in sight. The capitalist mode of production is characterised by the necessity of constant expansion.

> **"**
>
> Capitalism can no more be persuaded to limit growth than a human being can be persuaded to stop breathing
>
> **"**

MURRAY BOOKCHIN

Growth in this sense does not mean more time, health, happiness or contentment, but only the ever-expanding increase in profits. The idea of a fulfilled life is to savour as much as possible of what capitalist modernity has to offer, creating a purely consumer society. This is the basic paradigm of capitalist modernity: an imperialist, all-consuming, nature-destroying lifestyle.

The exploitation of nature and humanity to maximise the profits of a few has no moral limits. Social status is defined by power and wealth. Individualism and greed have become virtues. Disregard for everyone and everything is reflected in society's mentality and culture. It's accepted that development, be it human or natural, requires rivalry and competition. Profit and enrichment become the meaning of existence.

The current ecological crisis has shaken up the modern social-natural relationship, because the effects of trying to control and commodify nature have become obvious. But the strategy of capitalist modernity is now to make the ecological crisis itself the starting point of a renewed deepening of the exploitation and commodification of nature. Because, according to the experts and economists, whatever in nature doesn't have a price, can't be appreciated, and there will be no economic incentives to spare it.

This shows once again that a solution to the ecological crisis will only be possible with a fundamental change in mentality and the methods of production, and the overcoming of capitalist modernity itself. The solution lies in restoring a balanced relationship between nature and humanity, at all levels. In this sense, it is about the renewed, conscious development of a democratic-ecological society.

> **"**
>
> The ecological question is fundamentally solved as the system is repressed and a socialist social system develops. That does not mean you cannot do something for the environment right away. On the contrary, it is necessary to combine the fight for the environment with the struggle for a general social revolution...
>
> **"**

ABDULLAH ÖCALAN

SOCIAL ECOLOGY AS A WAY OUT OF CAPITALIST MODERNITY

Social ecology is the science of people's relationship with their natural and social environments. It examines how these relationships are shaped from different perspectives spanning classical scientific disciplines including anthropology, philosophy, history, archaeology, and social theory. It is not a purely descriptive theory: its crucial project is how the critical human-nature relationship can be reimagined and transformed.

In theorising a new understanding of the societal relationship to nature, social ecology offers decisive starting points: humanity developed through a natural process of evolution, in which, early on, there was neither opposition, competition nor submission between nature and human. In this process of social development and in the organisational forms that societies have adopted, there is a connection to natural evolution. We can think of pre-human nature – plants and animals – as "first nature", the active, turbulent substance of organic life that is developing toward greater complexity and differentiation arriving, finally, at "second nature" – human beings who are self-conscious and aware, able to intervene in the natural world.

The social and the natural permeate each other. As human beings, we will always have basic natural needs, even though these have been institutionalised in society through a variety of social forms. We must also understand the uniqueness of humanity's intellect in the interplay of natural and social evolution. The brain did not come from nowhere, but was the result of a long evolutionary process that slowly developed into a complex nervous system. The intellect is thus deeply rooted in nature. This uniqueness is characterised by the social behaviours of people, their creativity and imagination.

> **"**
>
> ...the human species is a warmhearted, exciting, versatile and especially intelligent way of life in which nature has testified to its highest creative power and is not merely a cold-blooded, genetically determined, thoughtless insect.
>
> **"**

MURRAY BOOKCHIN

In humans, nature has created a form of life that, through awareness and reason, can shape and change its environment. Unimaginable, limitless paths of evolution can open up before us. But humanity must also accept the responsibility that results from its creative power and this connection with the creative power of nature. This does not happen by denying our own productive and creative powers and placing them in opposition to the power of nature, by making a contrast between nature and society, or between living fertility and dead technology. Rather, we must see ourselves as integrated with nature, viewing nature as a realm of potentiality in which human beings represent the apex of nature's long evolution toward ever greater consciousness, subjectivity, creativity and freedom. "Humanity, in effect, becomes the potential voice of a nature rendered self-conscious and self-formative" (Bookchin). Human beings alone are able to intervene to change the course of the natural world through technology and innovation. The question is whether they will do it rationally, in the service of ever greater freedom, or destructively.

CORNERSTONE OF A DEMOCRATIC-ECOLOGICAL SOCIAL ORDER

If human alienation from its natural environment and ecological destruction cannot be separated from internal social conflicts, then social ecology must propose a new social order. Such an order must be based on radically democratic structures and built up outside of state power, which has always been a centralised structure of control.

Democracy is the antithesis to the state, dissociates itself from it and represents a self-organised regulation of the processes of societal self-coordination. In such a society, production of commodities can only take place in the sense of a cooperative, ecological and decentralised mode of production. Needs are determined based on a democratic process of negotiation and with the awareness of the possibilities of an ecological system in balance between nature and human beings. This means that technologies, modes of production, distribution, and forms of consumption will be decided upon in terms of their impact on the natural environment. At the same time, decisions must be evaluated on a longer-term basis. Often, ecological consequences can only be understood with a long-term perspective. The essential criterion is not only the protection of nature, but the improvement of the ecosystem and its equilibrium.

If the state and capitalist modernity derive their power from the creation of a hegemonic culture and mentality, then an ecological society must be a political and moral society that offers mutual aid, service to society and nature, and an active role in one's own self-determination.

In this society, humanity will regain an understanding of nature that has nearly been lost. And if capitalism alienated humanity from nature and from the land, then an ecological society must insist on love of the land, which houses people and gives them what they need to live. As Öcalan points out, "a life without the awareness of a nature that is alive and well, talking to us, living with us and living through it, [...] is hardly worth living".

A democratic-ecological society is based on the moment of reconciliation between humanity and nature, which lies only in the overcoming of domination over both. A fundamental prerequisite for this is to subdue capitalist modernity with its requirement of oppression, exploitation and accumulation – and eventually overcome it. The democratic-ecological society will enter into a new relationship with nature, to improve its beauty and diversity for future generations.

> "
>
> Social ecology advances
> a message that calls
> not only for a society
> free of hierarchy and
> hierarchical sensibilities,
> but for an ethics that
> places humanity in the
> natural world as an agent
> for rendering evolution
> social and natural fully
> self-conscious.
>
> "

MURRAY BOOKCHIN

CAPITALIST MODERNITY

The crisis in the relationship between humanity and nature

W ith the rise of capitalist systems of both finance and thought, industrialisation, centralisation and the increased exploitation of people and nature have taken hold almost everywhere in the world. This has often taken place through the mechanisms of coercion, robbery, resettlement and armed force. Access to the resources necessary for life is almost completely subjugated to the dictates of capital accumulation and centralism. The dream of turning everything into a commodity has even colonised life itself: corporations now use genetic engineering to bring the entire food chain under their command.

Capitalism has warped the environment and produced huge monocultures. This centralisation and the associated alienation of people from nature led to resistance early on, because small farmers did not want to give up their land. So centralisation and capitalisation of the supply of vital goods and energy required a justification strategy. They argued that the worldwide spread of the market economy of centralism and modern state bureaucracies emancipated people from the constraints of nature and brought humanity progress and global prosperity. The brutal poverty facing large parts of the world's population, the inability of the capitalist system to provide people with the necessities for life, and the reckless pace of extraction of natural resources all give the lie to these claims.

URBAN AND COUNTRYSIDE

Industrialisation, and the associated transition from the feudal to the capitalist mode of production, led and continues to lead to a worldwide exodus of former peasants to the cities, which grew to huge metropolises. Where urbanisation didn't happen by itself, it was enforced. More than half of the world's population already lives in cities, or the slums that surround them. The environmental, economic and psychological consequences of this concentration of people are enormous. Capitalist modernity is tearing apart both city and the countryside. The country, the origin of modern human society, is being relegated to the position of supplier for the city. In the richer parts of the world, the capitalist cities and metropolises of the West, people try to compensate for this deep lack and alienation with farm holidays, bamboo forests as their desktop wallpaper, or with a few tomato plants on the balcony. But the turmoil remains.

The mentality in the cities, even more so than in the countryside, is marked by individualism, commodification, consumption, and competition. The habitat becomes the commodity; those who have no money are displaced. Everyone rushes, faces are tired in the elevators, eyes avoid contact. This mentality, which has turned cities into places of cold isolation, is at the heart of the logic of neo-liberal capitalism.

FINITE RESOURCES

The machine of capital is kept running by competition – the principle of "all against all" – and by the constant compulsion to accumulate, i.e. to make more capital out of capital. Nature does not appear in the calculations of this economic and political system, but its exploitation is so intense today that it can no longer be ignored. For millions of years, humans and their ancestors did not dare remove more from nature than it could replace. Today, with capitalist modernity, all that has changed. By hunting and fishing on a massive scale, whole species have been nearly – and in some cases completely – exterminated; the bison herds have disappeared from North America, as have various whale species from Asian coasts. Nature has been demoted to a convenience store, a supplier of raw materials.

As whole generations grow up in corrugated steel huts between garbage dumps, the pollution of air and water is becoming an ever greater problem. Islands of garbage hundreds of miles in diameter collect in the oceans, while drinking water is increasingly contaminated with toxic substances. The government agencies of the world have still not found a solution for the storage of nuclear waste – most likely because there is no solution. One might be tempted to think that the false promises of capitalist modernity would finally become plain, at least on this point, but today more nuclear power plants are being built in China and other emerging economies than ever before.

As if the smog-filled mega-cities, overfishing, contaminated drinking water and poisoned food-supply-chains were not enough, the greatest catastrophe of all has now announced itself with ferocious force: climate change. It's one of the main effects of livestock cultivation, industry, and traffic. The Earth's climate is a delicately balanced system and has always been sensitive to changes; however, these changes have rarely led to major problems for the balance of nature, or the relationships between water, air, flora and fauna. Previous changes in the climate led to evolutionary adaptations in animals and plants to the changing living conditions in their ecosystem, thus contributing to greater diversity. But the sudden climate change caused by the capitalist mode of production reverses this trend, because flora and fauna cannot adapt quickly enough. More and more species die out, leading to global extinction of an extent that the Earth has not seen for sixty million years.

HOTHOUSE EARTH

The connection between greenhouse gases and the heating of the climate is well-known. These gases slow the escape of the sun's heat from the Earth, having the same effect as glass in a greenhouse. Greenhouse gases are not only produced by the combustion of coal, oil and gas in industry, vehicles, and heating systems, but also increasingly by livestock cultivation, whether in animal factories or on organic farms. Although the amount of methane gas released (in particular from cows, sheep and other ruminants) during digestion is less than the amount of carbon dioxide expelled from internal combustion engines, the impact of methane on the atmosphere is stronger than that of carbon dioxide.

Even if many people in the centres of capitalist modernity have lost the ability to notice changes in their local climate, the effects of climate change are felt directly by more and more people: glaciers are melting and natural catastrophes, including devastating storms, drought and forest fires, are more frequent. More and more regions in the southern hemisphere are drying up and deserts are spreading because of the lack of rain. It is clear that this is only the beginning. Already, so many greenhouse gases have been released into the atmosphere that even if no more were produced from tomorrow onwards, further heating would still be inevitable. By the end of this century, the world's atmosphere will have heated up by three to six degrees, with drastic effects on weather, flora and fauna.

Oil ponds created by the extraction of oil in Cizîrê Canton.

The world as we know it will soon be unrecognisable. The heating of the climate is leading to changes in the air currents and thus to ever more extreme weather conditions. As deserts spread in some regions, in others, floods and rainfall increase. Even the ocean currents, which rely on both heat differences and a sensitive freshwater and saltwater system, are affected by the higher rate of warming and melting of frozen freshwater reserves at the poles. Due to the massive disruption of the water flows, coasts with a hitherto mild climate could experience periods of cold in the next few decades as have not existed there for millennia. At the same time, previously snowy mountain slopes turn grey, and green forests turn to steppes.

The warming climate melts the ice at the South and North Poles, and the level of the ocean increases. Coastal villages and cities worldwide are threatened by rising sea levels and more frequent hurricanes. The heating of the climate increases disproportionately, at first slowly and then faster and faster. The melting of the polar ice caps is another reason for this: they function like a large mirror, as the white of the ice and snow reflects much of the sun's rays – the more the ice caps melt, the less sunlight they reflect and the faster the Earth heats up. The thawing of permafrost soils is another cause of an exponential rate of heating. These soils, common in Siberia and Alaska, have been frozen for tens of thousands of years and store huge amounts of methane gas. As the permafrost thaws, this gas is released into the atmosphere.

BURNING FORESTS

Another problem is the destruction of primeval forests, especially in South America and Asia. These forests store massive amounts of carbon dioxide. Through deforestation, this capacity for carbon dioxide storage is lost for decades. Additional carbon dioxide is released through slash-and-burn agriculture. In most cases, monocultures are planted on the burnt areas. These practices destroy the ecological balance, erode the soil, and make farms highly susceptible to pests (which are spreading because of the rise in heat, and the infestation by pests of weakened trees in neighbouring areas). Following the logic of so-called efficient production, more and more chemical fertilisers and insecticides are used, which poison the soil and water. Frequently, the burned areas are also used for livestock cultivation or for the production of forage crops like soy and corn for livestock, which compounds the problem.

Because the mechanisms of evolution are not adapted to the pace of anthropogenic climate change, experts around the world are trying to find ways to artificially adapt nature. But the race with the climate cannot be won. Because they know this, governments and the media are happy to spread dystopian images of the catastrophe that is approaching us. In shock, unable to maneuver, humanity bobs towards the abyss. What is usually overlooked is that we do not need to wait for the big catastrophe on day X, it is already here.

ABOVE AND BELOW

The destruction of our lives and livelihoods engenders a pessimistic view of humanity among many people. Humanity itself is declared an evil, which suggests that all human beings bear the same responsibility for the ecological catastrophe. Even the revelation of the catastrophe is turned into a lie, for it does not say who benefits from the exploitation of nature and who suffers. The contradiction of centres and periphery, of ruling and oppressed classes, is ignored.

Indigenous environmental struggles against habitat destruction, blockades of nuclear waste shipments, and demonstrations against overfishing have made it impossible for rulers to deny the impact of capitalist economics on nature or to sweep it under the carpet. Often, the peoples living more or less in harmony with their natural environment have been exploited, enslaved and massacred in tandem with the destruction of the environment that had sustained them. The rise of the capitalist centres of Europe and North America was built not only on the control of resources, trade routes and markets, but also on the dead bodies of indigenous peoples. The mass murders and genocides of hundreds of millions of indigenous people on the American, Asian and African continents have always been part of the struggle by imperialist centres for hegemony – for complete power over people and nature.

The colonial and neo-colonial wars were always wars against the natural society and nature itself. For many peoples of the world, the triumphant advance of capitalist modernity meant rape, burning forests, defoliation, and Agent Orange.

The Western missionaries' promises of salvation have not come to pass. For hundreds of millions of people the capitalist system has left only its garbage – the plastic bags littering the steppes of Africa have become a symbol of this. The poorer parts of the world's population, the global sub-proletariat, bear the brunt of climate change and environmental degradation. The societies of Africa, the Middle East and Southeast Asia, still reeling from wars, colonialism and neo-colonial exploitation, are those hit hardest by drought and other environmental disasters, even though they contribute a relatively small part of the greenhouse gases.

The more 'developed' a nation, the more destructive. For example, US greenhouse gas emissions are 50 times higher than Pakistan's, yet Pakistan, not the U.S., ranks among the top ten states that are affected by climate change. It is also the people in the so-called developing countries who are most affected by the ever-worsening water shortages. Water is already being used as a weapon in military and social conflicts, and wars over water resources will intensify.

Over the next few decades, tens of millions of people (especially in the global South) will have to leave their homes because increased drought, rising temperatures, and more frequent extreme weather events will destroy the basis for their agriculture and lead to yet more hunger and poverty. The richer centres in the global North, where the decisions are made about world markets, investment, social and ecological destruction, are stalling. For now, walls have been hastily erected around "Fortress Europe" and the United States as a shield against those who want to escape destroyed livelihoods.

THE LAST EXCUSE

But the walls cannot keep everyone out, and the natural and climatic catastrophes are now beginning to hit the capitalist centres themselves, so their rulers are desperately looking for solutions. And they are doing this with the same positivist methods that led to climate change and environmental destruction in the first place. The solution to the crisis becomes a mere question of the correct calculations and techniques. The crisis is to be solved by capital, even as it has been created by capital.

If you're clever, you can make a lot of money with renewable energy, electric cars and free-range eggs. On the billboards, the good news of the ruling class is written: "Go Green!" Many who used to take to the streets to demand the end of the destruction of nature, have become diverted by the idea of green capitalism, which attempts to claim a contradictory allegiance to both capital accumulation and nature.

When they say that nature can only be protected if everything in it has a price – a value under capitalism – the apologists for green capitalism follow the logic of exploitation over the defence of ecology. They claim to be able to slow down the degradation of nature, simply by making it more expensive. But commodification only deepens the catastrophe. Protecting nature becomes a luxury for the rich, who can greenwash their guilty conscience through organic products and electric cars. The market economy, no matter how many times it is painted green, pays attention to nature only as long as it pays off. Behind this green facade the destructive and dirty production continues. There is no fundamental change in the compulsion to compete or the exploitation of human labour power.

DECIDE

Instead of tackling the cause of the destruction of nature – capitalism itself – the symptoms are treated instead. The connections between the market economy, exploitation, destruction of nature, war and migration show what the result is when centralist and hierarchical systems try to subjugate nature. A solution that ignores these relationships, a solution within the existing system, is not possible; our survival will not be possible if we continue to live in a society where everything is made into a commodity, based on the private ownership of the means of production and land, with all its destructive consequences. Only the direct and democratic control of the means of production and land (and ecological resources) by the people can create a socio-ecological alternative.

Instead of hoping that the states of the world will provide us with solutions, we must act, together – civil society must lead the way. To wait any longer would be madness.

> "
>
> The connections between the market economy, exploitation, destruction of nature, war and migration show what the result is when centralist and hierarchical systems try to subjugate nature. A solution that ignores these relationships, a solution within the existing system, is not possible.
>
> "

INTERNATIONALIST
COMMUNE OF ROJAVA

To find a way out of the
dead end of the ecological
catastrophe brought about
by capitalist modernity
requires effort and the
courage to break new
ground. The first steps
have been taken, but the
need for a social-ecological
revolution means there is
still much to do.

INTERNATIONALIST
COMMUNE OF ROJAVA

ECOLOGICAL CHALLENGES IN ROJAVA

Perspectives for an ecological society

The Rojava region stretches along the Turkish-Syrian border, in the shadow of the Taurus Mountains, from Iraq almost to the Mediterranean Sea. In the south, the desert extends into the heart of Syria. The climatic zone in which Rojava is located is described as a steppe, between desert and a humid climate; it rains from October to April. With this climate, there are good conditions for agriculture. The areas along the banks of the Euphrates, Xabur and Tigris, as well as the entire canton of Afrîn, have fertile soils.

ROJAVA IN THE CONTEXT OF THE COLONIAL POLITICS OF SYRIA AND TURKEY

The consequences of the capitalist mentality and state violence against society and the environment are clearly visible in Rojava. The Ba'ath regime neither was nor is interested in an ecological society. Until 2012, Rojava was in a colonially dependent relationship with the Syrian Assad regime, which strongly affected the economic and environmental situation in the region. Maximum resource exploitation and high agricultural production rates were always given the highest priority. Both were geared for export to other regions of Syria and abroad. The systematic deforestation of forests enabled monocultures of wheat in the Cizire canton, of olives in Afrin, and a mix of both in Kobani. These monocultures shape the landscape of Rojava.

For decades it was forbidden to plant trees or grow vegetable gardens. Even today, the effects of this colonial policy are shaping people's lives and environment, creating a major contrast between Kurdish-majority and Arab majority cities and areas. The population was kept dependent by repressive politics and underdevelopment of the region, as well as the prohibition against growing food for their own use, and systematically forced to emigrate and provide cheap labor to surrounding Syrian metropolises, such as Aleppo, Raqqa and Homs. Many worked there in the regime-supported raw material processing industry, which was supplied with raw materials that were also from Rojava.

Energy production and consumption, inadequate waste disposal, and massive use of chemicals in agriculture have heavily polluted the soil, air and water. However, the people of Rojava and the Democratic Self-administration are not only struggling with the environmental legacy of the Ba'ath regime. Another serious threat is the hostile policy of the Turkish state against Rojava. In addition to military attacks, the constant threat of invasion and an economic embargo, the construction of dams in Turkish-occupied Northern Kurdistan and the massive extraction of groundwater for Turkish agriculture is a problem. As a result, there has been a dramatic decline in the amount of water flowing from the north to Rojavan rivers and a steady drop in the groundwater level. Moreover, it has been a common practice of the Turkish military for years to set fire to existing forests, especially olive trees in Afrîn Canton. One goal of this policy is to take away people's livelihood, both economically and ecologically, and thus force them to leave their land.

The policies of the Syrian regime have led to a growing alienation of Rojava's people from nature. The social knowledge and practice of organic farming, the cultivation of vegetables and the knowledge of local flora and fauna have been lost. Thus today, the lack of skills and initiative of the people to organise, to cultivate and to develop their land is a problem that the revolution in Rojava has to solve.

AGRICULTURE AND FORESTRY

Monoculture and chemical fertilization

From the perspective of short-term income maximisation, monocultures appear more productive and easier to farm; however, long-term studies show that monocultures deplete the soil because they have a negative impact on its nutrient composition. Nutrients are removed from the soil and, ultimately, lost forever. In addition, monocultures lead to increased pest rates and often pose a problem for the water supply due to soil desiccation – extreme drying through loss of moisture. This means monocultures generally require an artificial water supply and high quantities of fertiliser, which is often produced chemically. On a global scale, the use of chemical fertilisers has so degraded the soils on which they are used that this form of agriculture can only be practiced for about fifty more harvest phases. After that, the soil for the cultivation of food will simply be unusable. The return to an organic fertiliser-based agricultural system is unavoidable – it is a question of when, not if.

Monocultures also have a negative impact on ecological diversity, on the sensitive interaction of flora and fauna. To combat the increased infestation by yield-reducing insects, plants and fungi, chemical poisons are used which, in combination with the fertiliser, have a powerful negative impact on soil and water quality. These problems can be observed in Rojava, especially in the Cizîrê Canton, which has a strong focus on wheat cultivation – the wheat is grown along the Turkish-Syrian border in a belt about ten kilometres wide. In Afrîn, agriculture is heavily focused on monocultures of olive trees, a policy that was driven by the regime for two decades before the revolution. Old forest stands were cut down to facilitate olive cultivation, which also significantly affected ecological diversity.

Use of pesticides

The use of pesticides in Rojava has risen sharply in the last 20 years. They are still imported from Turkey and China, via the Syrian regime. Before the Rojava Revolution, the regime forced farmers to use pesticides. Today, the effects of this policy are becoming clear: although there are no official studies, diseases such as cancer are particularly prevalent in the predominantly Kurdish-inhabited regions of Syria. This is almost certainly due to the high use of carcinogenic pesticides. Often the ingredients in the pesticides and their proper use were not specified. This was especially true of pesticides from Turkey, which were forced off their own domestic market because of harmful ingredients, but which continued to be exported to Syria and used in Rojava, in a practice known as "dumping."

Agricultural pests

Rojavan agriculture is affected by various pests, which has meant a reliance on pesticide use. The biggest problems are Colorado potato beetles, grasshoppers, and fungal infestations. These pests are not originally from Syria, but were imported; it's believed that the Turkish government is deliberately promoting the spread of pests from agricultural land in Turkey/Northern Kurdistan to Rojava, using chemicals that do not kill the pests but push them south into the nearby fields in Rojava.

QAMISHLI

Rojava is one of the most agriculturally important regions of Syria. Production is mainly grain, cotton and olives.

LAND UTILISATION IN SYRIA

■ Cultivated land with livestock; emphasis on grains, cotton, fruits and olives

■ Forest

■ Steppe land with nomadic herding (sheep) and scattered cultivation

■ Desert and steppe lands with some nomadic herding

Cotton

Olives

Fruit

Wheat

Tobacco

Sustainable water use and diversification of agriculture according to the needs of the people

Organic farming in Rojava is not possible without overcoming monocultures and reducing water consumption. The Agricultural Protection Committee has taken a number of measures to diversify agricultural use and to promote the sustainable use of water.

To control the extraction of groundwater, all water wells were registered by the committee and further drilling of wells for agricultural use was prohibited. In addition, only 60 per cent of agricultural areas may be planted with crops requiring irrigation. These measures also have a positive effect on the diversification of agriculture, as more varieties of crops that require no additional irrigation are now being planted. These include lentils, chickpeas and beans. The cultivation of these types of crops now accounts for about 25 per cent of total agricultural land. Another 15 per cent is planted with vegetables and cotton, which require intensive irrigation. The largest part, around 50 per cent, will continue to be sown with wheat. The remaining 10 per cent is left fallow and allowed to regenerate for a year. In addition, farmers are encouraged to alternate the crops they plant, so that the soil can replenish itself. Although there is still a strong emphasis on the cultivation of wheat, a real difference can be seen from a few years ago, when crops such as lentils and beans accounted for no more than 10 per cent of the area.

In Afrîn, projects to diversify agriculture have also been promoted since the beginning of the revolution. Mango, grape and citrus fruit trees, which suit Afrîn's Mediterranean climate, have been planted.

Another crucial change in Rojava's agriculture is the orientation of production toward local consumption and away from exports, both to other parts of Syria and abroad. For example, cotton cultivation has been reduced and vegetable cultivation increased. The canton of Cizîrê no longer exports food from Rojava, but does send some to the other cantons in Rojava – Afrîn and Kobanî – as well as to areas in need of help that have recently been liberated from the Islamic State.

Agroforestry

A system of different combinations of crops can address environmental problems caused by monoculture and increase yields – and a combination of field and tree crops can also help. This combination of agriculture and forestry is known as Agroforestry.

Agroforestry provides more habitat for animals and reduces erosion. Tree roots ensure the penetration of water into the soil, thus helping to ameliorate the lowering groundwater table. At the same time, trees reduce the amount of fertiliser necessary for the grain. The root system pulls nutrients and water from deeper layers of the soil upwards; with leaf fall, these nutrients re-enter the topsoil and are then taken up by the crops.

Cultivation of poplars and wheat or other cereals is practised in subtropical latitudes like Rojava's. Agroforestry can be practiced even in smaller units such as city gardens. Layers of vegetation at different heights ensure optimal light reception and enable an increase in yields, in a relatively small space. Through an intelligent selection of cooperating plant communities, forest gardens can be built up. Ecological diversity also ensures flexibility and stability.

Urban agriculture: autonomy and food security in urban areas

Urban agriculture – planting former commercial or industrial sites in cities or rooftop gardens – could help decentralise Rojava's agricultural system. The city's fruit and vegetable needs, as well as the removal of its organic waste, can both be dealt with in this way. Decentralising some food production to households and communities in urban areas also increases their autonomy and provides improved food security. A good example is the Cuban capital Havana, where about 90 per cent of the fruit and vegetables consumed are cultivated in the city itself, and the small-scale urban agricultural areas are fertilised with organic household waste.

Nature reserves and afforestation - improving water quality and preserving biodiversity

The creation and preservation of nature reserves is one of the central activities of the Committee for Nature Conservation in the canton of Cizîrê. In the canton of

Cizîrê, two protected areas have already been established: Hayaka, around Lake Sefan, and Mizgefta Nû.

Farming, hunting and fishing have been banned in the nature reserves. The ban now contributes to the improvement of drinking water quality, as well as the protection of various animal and plant species. A significant project in the nature reserves, and beyond, is reforestation in both rural and urban areas. In 2016 and 2017, the Conservation Area Committee planted some 8,000 trees, including in the Hayaka and Mizgefta Nu Nature Reserves and in the cities of Çilaxa and Hesekê. In the Hayaka Conservation Area, afforestation of a further 100,000 trees is planned for the next few years.

WATER SCARCITY, WATER POLLUTION AND POSSIBLE SOLUTIONS

Water shortage in Rojava

The drinking-water supply to towns and villages comes mostly from springs and lakes. In the canton of Cizîrê, Lake Sefan supplies the cities of Dêrîk and Qamislo.

The supply of water for both household and agricultural use is one of the central problems in Rojava. Climate change has meant less rain and a shortening of the rainy season. Since the1990s, precipitation in the Cizîrê region has fallen by around 10 to 15 per cent. Turkey's policy of cutting off the water supply to Rojava, severely restricts the flow of water in the main rivers (such as the Euphrates and Xabur). In addition, many new wells have been dug in Turkey/Northern Kurdistan; this excessive use of water in both Turkey and Rojava, has seen the groundwater level drop significantly in recent decades. There are more than 30,000 wells in use in the canton of Cizîrê alone, and despite the attempt to register all of them, it can be assumed that this number is actually higher.

Only a few years ago, groundwater could be extracted from an average depth of 100 metres: it has now it has dropped to around 150 metres. The scarcity of groundwater has been exacerbated by water-intensive agriculture; as a result, the rivers in Rojava are running low on water, which has contributed to the dying off of forested areas along the river banks. Again, this only exacerbates the problem of water-capture.

The Islamic State (IS) has also contributed to the problem of water scarcity: as they were pushed back, IS blocked off springs and wells. This was a deliberate, vindictive policy of IS to harm the population and its agriculture, even in defeat.

The situation of the Xabûr river, which was the main water supply for the cities of Til Abiyad (Girê Spî) and Hesekê as well as for the agriculture in the surrounding region, is a good example of various converging problems: Turkey has brought the river flow almost to a stop; IS closed off other inflow sources; and locally introduced waste has heavily contaminated the water.

Water pollution and possible alternatives

Much wastewater in Rojava ends up in rivers, which is extracted for use in agricultural irrigation. Dumping of wastewater in rivers is also common in Northern Kurdistan. For example, the city of Nisêybîn, with a population of 100,000, puts its untreated waste into the Chax Chax River, which then flows through the city of Qamislo.

The uncontrolled discharge of wastewater and its subsequent use in agriculture is often a cause of disease and affects the ecological systems of the rivers; however, if properly treated, the wastewater could be made safe for agricultural use. Timely separation of grey-water (wastewater from sinks, showers etc.) and black-water (wastewater from toilets) makes this process a lot simpler. The use of grey-water is of particular importance to Rojava, as water supply is a problem in many regions and dependence on the policies of the Turkish state makes it difficult to improve the situation.

The use of grey-water in agriculture can also increase production. The required treatment level of grey-water prior to further use is decided on the basis of planned use. For example, it is possible to use grey-water for watering trees after a simple coarse filtration through a sieve. With a more intensive filtering through sand or similar material, the grey-water could also be used for the irrigation of crops.

Particularly in countries with high water scarcity, the use of grey-water is becoming increasingly important. For

Water pollution through oil extraction in Cizîrê Canton.

example, in parts of Australia, grey-water segregation is now legally required. Grey-water reuse not only reduces total water consumption, but also avoids the pollution of soil and rivers.

The use of black water for fertilization

Human waste is the largest source of nutrients available to agriculture from organic waste. The Stockholm Environment Institute estimates that one person's organic waste would be enough to grow 230 kilograms of grain annually. Urine is richer in nutrients (especially nitrogen) and more versatile, so it can be used on any kind of crop. Excrement also contains many nutrients and is excellent for improving soils; however, without a long composting, it should only be used to fertilise trees, shrubs, or grain for animal feed. After composting for at least a year, it can also be safely used to fertilise crops intended for human consumption.

The agricultural use of excrement also prevents it from entering the water, which is unavoidable with most conventional sewerage systems, and a major cause of pollution and disease. Once solid waste is mixed with water or urine, the resulting black-water becomes more difficult to treat. Treatment in most sewage systems focuses on re-separating the solid and liquid materials. Black-water can also be used for composting and, after a reasonable amount of time, the compost would also be suitable for use in crops intended for human consumption.

There are many examples worldwide of the use of human waste as agricultural fertiliser. According to research by the South China Agricultural University, organic fertiliser was the main source of fertiliser in China until the 1980s, and about 30 per cent of fertiliser used in the country still comes from human waste. The problems associated with both chemical fertilisers and the search for alternatives to the resulting increase in wastewater prompted the authorities to begin returning to organic in the early 2000s. The collection of urine supplies the fertiliser for urban agriculture throughout China, and much urban sewage is transported to agricultural areas in pipes or tankers. In the city of Dongsheng new flats have urine-separating dry toilets. Excrement is disposed in buckets and used for compost, the urine is stored in tanks and directly used as fertiliser.

In Sweden, intensive research is being done on ecological sanitation and various systems have already been put in place. Since 2002, the Swedish municipality of Tanum (average population 36,000) has introduced an ecological hygiene policy that promotes the use of dry toilets and urine separation. The urine is stored in tanks and then delivered by tanker to local farmers, along with black-water from septic tanks. The municipality of Trosa (11,000 inhabitants) near Stockholm stores its black-water for six months and then delivers it to farms outside the city, where it is used as fertiliser.

ENERGY PRODUCTION BETWEEN RENEWABLE ENERGIES AND FOSSIL FUELS

Petroleum extraction and processing:

Most of Syria's oil fields are in Rojava, especially in Cizîrê Canton. As the policy of the regime was to locate all manufacturing industries in the metropolises of Syria, the processing of crude oil into fuel did not take place in Rojava but rather in the regime's industrial centres. With the revolution, Rojavan oil refining began. The biggest fuel needs are for emergency electricity (from small generators) and transport. In winter, diesel is also used to generate heat in household stoves.

Today, about 5 per cent of all oil produced in the Middle East comes from Rojavan fields; however, due to the lack of parts and the embargo, this production is conducted at a very low level technically. Since current demand exceeds the capacity of the existing refineries, much of the crude oil is processed only to a very basic level. This reinforces the negative impact of the already heavily polluting oil industry. Thus, production and transport are associated with pollution of the environment, soil, water and air. This damage is particularly visible in the ponds created by the extraction and processing of the oil. There are currently no technically or financially feasible methods for avoiding this ecological burden available in Rojava.

Electricity production

Electricity production in Rojava is based on three sources: hydroelectric power plants, natural gas, and the electricity supply based on diesel generators run at the communal level. The general production by power plants is roughly divided into approximately 75 per cent hydro, and 25 per cent natural gas (the by-product of oil extraction), although this ratio fluctuates. Most parts of Rojava don't have sufficient electricity. In cities like Dêrîk, electricity is only available for six hours a day, while in other cities, such as Kobanî, it's twelve hours. Despite the additional power supply within the communes, a permanent and nationwide supply is currently not possible.

The mainstays of Rojavan power generation are the hydroelectric power plants, which are operated at the Tischrin and Tabqa dams on the Euphrates. The electricity is then transferred to the cities via long power lines. Theoretically, full power supply for Rojava would be possible from the existing hydropower plants if they were operated at full capacity – but they're not, for two reasons.

First, there is a lack of parts necessary for the repair of the plants. The war in Syria, which has been raging for more than seven years, has severely affected these vital power generation systems. The destroyed infrastructure, power lines, and substations still prevent the full supply of electricity to many regions of Rojava. Their reconstruction is a difficult undertaking given the economic embargo and the lack of financial resources.

Secondly, electricity generation is heavily dependent on the water policy of the Turkish state, because the key rivers have their sources in Turkey. In recent years, the Turkish government has increasingly promoted the construction of dams, which has had a profoundly detrimental impact on Syria's water supply – and which consolidates and expands Turkish geopolitical power. Despite contractual agreements between the Syrian and Turkish governments for the passage of fixed amounts of water, Turkey uses its control of water to influence political developments in Syria. Since the democratic forces in northern Syria (supported by the political structures of the Kurdish liberation movement) have put their system of democratic self-government into practice, the policy of the Turkish government has become even more restrictive.

The ecological and health consequences of the use of fossil fuels for heat and power generation, combined with unreliability of water flow based on the power politics of the Turkish state, is yet another reason for the decentralisation of energy production

Renewable energy and ecological construction

The geographical position of Rojava and the climatic conditions in the region make it suitable for various forms of renewable energy production.

Inexpensive and simple systems of water heating by solar artery systems on roofs, power generation by solar energy with photovoltaic technology, wind energy etc. could be the first steps in a decentralised energy system. This would reduce people's dependency on both the centralised hydro-electricity system and fossil fuels.

The way buildings are built plays an important role in saving energy: the less energy consumed, the less must be produced. In Rojava, many smaller buildings are made of natural materials such as clay, wood and stone, which, compared to standard building materials like concrete, steel and cement, cause less pollution and use less energy during manufacture. In addition, this ecological construction is about one-third cheaper than conventional architecture. Houses that are built in this way are also easier to cool in the summer and to heat in the winter, cutting down on power and fuel costs.

WASTE DISPOSAL, RECYCLING AND COMPOSTING

Recycling

In recent years, a functioning waste disposal system has been set up in most of the cities of Rojava. The waste is brought from individual households or streets to nearby landfills and burned there. No municipal waste separation or recycling system exists in Rojava. As a result, water and soil quality are severely impacted, leading to health problems (especially in children). The particles that are created during the incineration of the waste pollute soil and water and spread through the air, including to agricultural land, where they enter the food chain.

Recycling is an alternative to this form of waste disposal, and some projects are currently being considered by the self-government bodies, including a paper recycling plant. This would involve separation of paper waste from other types of refuse at the household level, which would be re-used in paper-making. The project, estimated to cost $70 million (U.S.), is still in its infancy because of the lack of funding.

There are also much simpler and cheaper methods of recycling. The recycling of hard plastic, for example, is not complicated and can be done with simple machines. This enables small-scale and decentralised forms of recycling that are already practiced in many parts of the world.

Composting: organic fertilizer for rural and urban agriculture

The use of organic waste also plays an important role in an ecological society. Animal manure is already used in agriculture in Rojava; however, this use can and should be expanded. The chemical fertiliser used in Rojava costs $35 million (U.S.) a year. All this chemical fertiliser must be imported, and this creates a significant dependency on the various regimes in the region. More efficient recycling of organic waste would greatly reduce – if not entirely eliminate – the need to import chemical fertiliser, increase agricultural production, and increase farmer autonomy. From a global perspective, the transition from chemical to organic fertiliser must be done as soon as possible: without fundamental changes, the current form of agriculture canonly be practiced for about the next fifty harvest phases.

Composting requires the creation of favourable conditions for the decomposition of organic waste into biologically stable humic substances, which can then be used for agriculture and forestry. In addition to its nutrient content, compost increases soil fertility by improving soil structure (improving the mobility of air, water and nutrients in the soil), adding beneficial microbes, and increasing the availability of nutrients. The use of organic waste for agriculture is common in many countries, and simple precautions can minimise any potential health risks. Its use in agriculture and forestry saves money, prevents soil erosion, and reduces pollution. Composting is of particular strategic importance to a society whose access to chemical fertiliser can be easily curtailed by governments and corporations.

About 50 per cent of all household waste is organic. On average, every person produces around half a kilogram of compostable waste per day. After the natural processes of composting, this amount is reduced to 50 grams of ready-made compost. Small-scale composting in individual households is easier in rural areas but also possible in cities. This is particularly the case when used in conjunction with urban farming – as in Cuba, where it is an important part of the country's food production. It is also possible to develop large-scale composting facilities for rural agriculture. This is common in Western countries, where household organic waste is collected and converted into agricultural compost. For a city the size of Dêrîk (with a population of about 40,000 people), this would mean a daily intake of 20 tonnes of organic waste for the daily production of two tonnes of finished compost.

There are many different types of composting systems, such as simple compost piles or boxes. As long as certain conditions (including temperature and humidity) are regularly checked and adjusted if necessary, the compost will decompose until it is ready for use.

TRAFFIC AND AIR POLLUTION

The majority of diesel and gasoline consumption in Rojava is for transport, which is also the main source of air pollution, especially in the larger cities. The expansion of public transport is one way of minimising this impact.

Urban air quality can also be improved by planting trees. One of the central strategies of municipalities, in collaboration with the committees responsible for ecology, is to plant more trees in urban areas, and to maintain existing ones. Current projects include the planting of one of the main thoroughfares in the city of Qamislo, which will cost $60,000. In the city of Tabqa, which was liberated from IS in the summer of 2017, a campaign will be started this year to replace the urban tree stock, 75 per cent of which has dried up or been totally destroyed. This damage to the

Traffic and air pollution
in the city of Qamishlo.

tree population has its roots in the failed policies of the city administration under the Syrian regime. The war in urban areas also had an impact on the stock of trees at the municipal level. Because of the climate and water shortage reforestation is a labour-intensive process.

Projects such as these provide better urban air quality, give shade in the summer months (when temperatures can rise to 50 degrees Celsius or about 120 degrees Fahrenheit), create living spaces for birds, and improve the quality of life in general. As part of the ecological work of the self-government, the communes and local populations in the canton of Cizîrê are currently being surveyed about their particular needs for trees. More trees will then be planted in communities on the strength of this information.

EFFECTS OF THE WAR

The effects of the war on the ecological situation in Rojava have been considerable, in particular the pollution of the soil and water by ammunition. The use of depleted uranium shells by the international coalition causes severe health problems, and their residue lingers in the environment for a long time. Mortar ammunition, rockets and other explosive weapons include heavy metals and TNT, which are carcinogenic. When these weapons were used in urban areas, e.g. in Kobanî and

Hesekê, these substances mixed with dust from the destroyed buildings and found their way into citizens' respiratory tracts, into the water, and onto agricultural land. From there they found their way into the food. The long-term consequences are as yet unknown.

One of the Islamic State's tactics for protecting itself from air raids was to start large fires with thick smoke. These were produced by the burning of oil, along with other materials such as plastics, which heavily polluted the air, soil and water.

Further pollution of the air, water and soil resulted from the destruction of industrial facilities, which released toxic gases and chemicals. Though the impact this will have on Rojava remains to be seen, estimates by the non-governmental organisation PAX claim this burden on the environment will have long-term health effects.

ROJAVA – A DEMOCRATIC ECOLOGICAL SOCIETY UNDER CONSTRUCTION

Local self-sufficiency and cooperatives "collectivise our land, water and energy" (Öcalan) The relationships between production and use, city and country, centre and periphery, must be rethought and redesigned to build an ecological society. In Rojavan society, a cooperative, ecological and decentralised mode of production is the goal. All assets, or natural resources, must be socialised, and the economy democratised. It is crucial that production be decided on the basis of a democratic process of negotiation. It must be based on the possibilities of an intact, balanced ecological system and on the capabilities of the people themselves.

The communes are based on collective self-sufficiency. This eliminates the separation between the places of production and use, reduces long transport routes, and guarantees security of supply to the people. Also, it allows for the growth and retention of collective knowledge about agriculture, treatment and harvest.

In contrast to capitalist modes of production, cooperatives are able to produce according to people's needs, since they need not be subject to the logic of constant growth and profit maximisation. It is also possible for them to take into account long-term consequences for the natural world and design production with this in mind; indeed, care for the community is one of the seven cooperative principles. In cooperative forms of economics, knowledge is shared among people working together, as there is no classical separation or hierarchy of individual work steps, but rather a holistic approach.

The Rojavan system builds on community self-government in communes and production in cooperatives. It's intended that all resources, such as water, energy and land, become common goods. There are already 57 cooperatives, comprising around 8,700 families, in Cizîrê Canton alone.

Between claim and reality -
Rojava and the ecological society

The environmental challenges in Rojava/Northern Syria are enormous. Rojava exemplifies how ecological problems are interwoven with social and economic issues, how centralisation, capitalist economics, and the exploitation of humans and nature are interconnected.

For the foreseeable future, some contradictions cannot be resolved, but the negative effects can be minimised in the short term and the population can be informed about the dangers. Appropriate measures can be implemented without major investments of resources or money. The measures taken by the structures of the democratic self-administration for dealing with the ecological problems aim at the protection of existing ecosystems, reforestation, and the strengthening of ecological awareness. These are first steps, but they are far from sufficient.

We have shown some of the processes that would move the communes in Rojava closer to democratic autonomy in an ecological and decentralised way. To find a way out of the dead end of the ecological catastrophe brought about by capitalist modernity requires effort and the courage to break new ground. The first steps have been taken, but the need for a social-ecological revolution means there is still much to do.

MAKE ROJAVA
GREEN AGAIN

The "Make Rojava Green Again" campaign was launched in early 2018 by the Internationalist Commune of Rojava, in cooperation with the Committee for Natural Reserves (of the Commission for Economy), and the Committee for Ecology (of the Commission for Municipalities and Ecology of the self-administration in Rojava) with the aim of supporting and developing the ecological society in northern Syria. The campaign has three strands: education, practical works, and the organisation of global solidarity.

Education

The development of an ecological and democratic consciousness is the basis for understanding the balance between humanity and nature. It is about more than just scientific knowledge and a rational understanding: in order to overcome the alienation of people from nature, and thus from themselves, humanity today must go back to nature, to experience and appreciate it in order to protect it. For this reason, theoretical and educational work at all levels of society as well as concrete experiences in and with nature will be essential parts in the construction of an ecological society.

Education for internationalists

The Internationalist Academy, which has been under construction since the summer of 2017, will be the centre of our educational work. Here, internationalists can be trained according to the principles of radical democracy, women's liberation, and ecology, and prepared for work in Rojavan society through intensive language and cultural education. There will be lectures, seminars and discussions about the necessity for the ecological society, what it could look like, and what steps will be necessary to achieve it. Complementing the theoretical training at the Academy, all internationalists will get the chance to develop a true sense of nature through physical work in the affiliated tree cooperative and the reforestation projects we support. The practical work with the soil, and the handling and care of the plants and animals in the academy and tree nursery, will show the possibilities and the beauty – of a life in harmony with nature. With the help of internationalists, we want to develop an environmentally-conscious mentality and an understanding and practical knowledge of ecological living, both among ourselves and throughout the political structures and society of Rojava.

The Academy (which, along with the life and work within it, is still under construction) is designed according to ecological principles. How best to utilise water, soil, air, energy and waste is not only discussed theoretically, but also actually implemented. In doing so, we want to minimise our own contribution to pollution as well as become an example to similar projects working for a more ecological Rojava.

Education in society

Internationalists will work with the local structures to organise education for the development of ecological awareness and knowledge. It will take place in schools, youth centres, municipalities, communes and other institutions. This part of the curriculum will also involve leaving the classroom: trips to the Hayaka nature reserve, participation in planting work, and the establishment of school gardens will make nature more vital and relevant.

Afforestation of the Academy grounds

In autumn 2018, we are going to begin the afforestation of the Academy grounds. 7,200 square meters to the west, north, and east of the Academy will be planted with 2,000 trees, mostly pines and fruit trees, such as apple, pistachio, pomegranate, cherry, pear, fig and apricot. These will be irrigated and fertilised with the grey-water and organic fertiliser produced in the Academy itself. Over the next few years, olives, grapes and oak trees will be planted in an area of 12,500 square meters on the rocky slope to the south of the Academy, thus creating a forest that protects the environment and provides a safe haven for local flora and fauna.

Selecting seeds in a tree nursery in Qamishlo.

Waste management and recycling

Separation is the basis of waste management at the Academy. Organic waste (such as leftover food and paper) is immediately separated from non-organic waste (such as plastic or metal). Avoiding mixing the waste eliminates the unpleasant and time-consuming task of re-separating them later. The non-organic waste is further subdivided by type.

Instead of burning or burying the inorganic waste and polluting water, air and soil, the waste is separated and stored. The first separation is between waste that poses a direct hazard to water and soil, such as batteries or electronic waste, and non-hazardous plastic or metal waste. Hazardous waste is stored away from where it could contaminate water sources. The non-hazardous, non-organic waste is cleaned for hygiene reasons and also stored. Plans are underway to recycle plastic and metal waste, either on the Academy site itself or in future joint projects with the democratic self-administration structures.

The organic waste produced by the Academy is converted into fertiliser and used. This avoids hygiene problems that arise when this waste is disposed of in landfills, and also saves costs incurred by the purchase of chemical fertiliser. Food leftovers, paper and cardboard are collected and composted. After a few months, the compost turns into nutrient-rich humus that can be used to fertilise trees and vegetables on the Academy grounds. The Academy is expected to produce around ten tonnes of organic waste each year, which in turn will produce around one tonne of humus. The grey-water from our sinks and showers will also be used for irrigation and fertiliser, and the dry toilet system reduces the amount of black-water produced, allowing for the ecological use of the resulting waste as fertiliser.

Water management

Drinking water comes from a well in the Academy grounds. The wastewater can be divided into two categories: grey-water (i.e. the water from showers, the kitchen etc.) and black-water from the toilets. Most of the Academy's grey-water is collected and used for both irrigation and fertilisation. This prevents pollution and saves water and fertiliser. The grey-water is first sent to a tank where sediment and grease is filtered out. From there, the water flows to another tank, where it is stored for use. The grey-water is then used, mainly for watering the trees. This system saves around 2,500 litres of water a day. The black-water produced is stored in a separate tank. The research on the technical implementation and use of black-water as a fertiliser at the Academy is still ongoing.

Practical works

Although knowledge transfer and creation of ecological awareness will certainly be one of the strategic works in the process of building the ecological society, these educational activities must be followed by concrete steps. One of the biggest problems in Rojava is the lack of forests, which has a negative effect on air quality, soil erosion, the increasing

First grapevine planting in the garden of the Internationalist Academy.

water shortage, and the economic and psychological wellbeing of the population. The planting of trees is a solution to many pressing issues: it reduces soil erosion by wind and water and preserves the fertility of surrounding agricultural land; in areas such as the Hayaka Nature Reserve, reforestation also serves to protect watersheds and restore biodiversity. While economic activities such as timber production or agroforestry can play a role, in the long term, a massive reduction of CO_2 to reduce the greenhouse effect is vital for all humanity. To make all this possible, a lot of work is needed in Rojava; lost knowledge, lack of awareness, and economic challenges call for systematic and practical solutions.

The tree cooperative

An essential part of the ecological strategy of the self-administration in Rojava is the development of tree nurseries. Most existing nurseries in northern Syria are owned by private companies, making planting trees an expensive affair for many.

To help solve this problem, we started the construction of a nursery on the grounds of the Internationalist Academy. In 2018 alone, more than 50,000 shoots will be planted and raised on an area of 5,000 square metres. The focus will be on fruit trees, with a special emphasis given to plants that are tolerant of arid conditions, such as olive and oak. The nursery will provide both the Hayaka Nature Reserve and the local political structures (such as communities, cooperatives, institutions and municipalities) with trees and other plants. It will also be a place for practical research. Through targeted interventions and the use of alternative methods and technologies in the areas of water use, fertilisation and recycling, we will contribute to the reforestation of Rojava.

The nursery will be organised as a non-profit cooperative and the work there will be part of the training at the Internationalist Academy. All internationalists will contribute their labour power to the reforestation project. This will allow us to deliver trees at an affordable price. Our goal is to provide trees at about half of the cost of those from profit-oriented nurseries. The surplus of the tree cooperative, after deducting all costs such as transport, technology, construction, tools and working materials, will be invested in the expansion of the nursery (25%); the works of the Internationalist Academy (25%); and in the reforestation of the Hayaka Nature Reserve (50%).

The Hayaka Nature Reserve

The nature reserve of Hayaka is a few kilometres west of the town of Dêrîk, in Cizîrê Canton. It is named after the adjacent village and comprises a mainly poplar-covered forest area of more than 200 hectares and the Lake Sefan reservoir, which was created in the 1990s by the damming of 31 different source streams. Many wildlife and plant species that have been displaced by deforestation and monoculture have found refuge in Hayaka Nature Reserve. Despite habitat loss and hunting, wolves, foxes, wild pigs,

Growing zucchini seeds
in the greenhouse.

many different species of birds and other small animals were able to survive in the small forest areas around the lake. To preserve this natural biodiversity and some of the last forest in the region, the democratic self-administration declared the area a nature reserve in 2014. Hunting, fishing, construction of buildings, and agriculture were prohibited in the reserve. At the same time, the afforestation of the lakeshore began, with a long-term plan to plant more than 100,000 trees around the lake, over a length of 14 kilometres. Work is also being done to establish beekeeping in the reserve, and to make the variety of herbs available there accessible for medical research.

The preservation, expansion and continued afforestation of the Hayaka Nature Reserve is an integral part of the campaign. Both through the practical work of internationalists in the nature reserve and through financial support of the reforestation, we want to develop an ecological perspective for the region that encompasses the local population and their economic needs.

Organisation of worldwide solidarity

The third main aspect of the Make Rojava Green Again campaign will be the organisation of global solidarity. Through our campaign and outreach, we want to build a bridge between the local communal entities of the democratic self-administration and ecological projects in northern Syria, and interested activists, experts, academics, institutions and organisations from all over the world. Of course, one of the best ways to promote this ecological work is to get involved here in Rojava. But this possibility is not open to all people: coming to Rojava is difficult because of the political situation in the surrounding countries, and sometimes the route is completely closed. That's why several months should be planned for any stay in northern Syria. Nevertheless, there are many ways to help: whether in Rojava itself or from outside, solidarity and the struggle for an ecological society know no borders.

Financial support of the works

Although many of the ecological works in Rojava, as well as the work of the internationalists in the tree cooperative and the Hayaka Nature Reserve, are voluntary and unpaid, we, like the other local structures, depend on financial resources. Technology, machinery, tools, materials and transport costs, as well as wages for skilled local labor, cost money. If you want to strengthen the campaign and other ecological projects in northern Syria and safeguard them over the long term, you can contribute to building the ecological society through financial support. To give the projects more planning security, regular monthly donations are even better and are greatly appreciated. All donations will be used to build, maintain and further develop ecological projects in Rojava, beginning with the tree cooperative and support for the Hayaka Nature Reserve.

Nature at the environs of the
Internationalist Academy.

Knowledge exchange, project development, and ideas for an ecological Rojava

In northern Syria, there is a great need for more ecological awareness, expert knowledge, and committed scientists. Possibilities include remote video exchange, the training of Rojavan specialists here or abroad, or direct work on projects in northern Syria. Just as the world can learn from Rojava in many ways, Rojava also has much to learn from the world. That is why we are looking for interested and committed activists, experts, people with technical skills, and scientists with ideas for planning and implementing ecological projects in northern Syria and for developing a more ecological Rojava. In particular, we are looking for people with expertise and experience in the following areas:

- Sustainable forestry and agriculture in semi-arid regions
- Water use and sanitation
- Ecological sustainability and renewable energies
- Mechanical and electrical engineering
- Physics, chemistry and biology (and especially botany).

EPILOGUE

There is not much that we want to say at the end of this book. Our discussions and work are only just beginning and do not allow us to say much about successes and accomplishments.

However, we hope that we can contribute to finding ways out of the ecological crisis of our time. In the face of this crisis, so much seems lost and irrevocable. But we believe that people can make life better with their creative power, their understanding of justice, and their will to change. One of the more important aims of this book is to express this confidence.

For us, the planting of trees symbolises this will to contribute to the construction of an ecological society, a contribution whose results won't be visible in a year or two, but will go beyond the life of the individual and be our gift to future generations.

This book is an invitation to participate in our work: to be part of building an ecological society in Rojava and bringing international solidarity to life.

APPENDIX

The 7 Cooperative Principles

Cooperatives are based on the values of self-help, self-responsibility, democracy, equality, equity and solidarity. In the tradition of their founders, cooperative members believe in the ethical values of honesty, openness, social responsibility and caring for others. All cooperatives are guided by seven Cooperative Principles.

The Cooperative Principles are sometimes known as the Rochdale Principles, named after early advocates of the cooperative movement, the Rochdale Pioneers (1844). The International Co-operative Alliance (ICA) is an independent, non-governmental organisation established in 1895 to unite, represent and serve cooperatives worldwide. In 1995 the ICA updated the cooperative principles, and today the principles followed by all cooperatives worldwide are:

1. Voluntary and Open Membership

Cooperatives are voluntary organisations, open to all persons able to use their services and willing to accept the responsibilities of membership, without gender, social, racial, political or religious discrimination.

2. Democratic Member Control

Cooperatives are democratic organisations controlled by their members, who actively participate in setting their policies and making decisions. Men and women serving as elected representatives are accountable to the membership. In primary cooperatives members have equal voting rights (one member, one vote) and co-operatives at other levels are also organised in a democratic manner.

3. Member Economic Participation

Members contribute equitably to, and democratically control, the capital of their cooperative. At least part of that capital is usually the common property of the cooperative. Members usually receive limited compensation, if any, on capital subscribed as a condition of membership. Members allocate surpluses for any or all of the following purposes: developing their cooperative, possibly by setting up reserves, part of which at least would be indivisible; benefiting members in proportion to their transactions with the cooperative; and supporting other activities approved by the membership.

4. Autonomy and Independence

Cooperatives are autonomous, self-help organisations controlled by their members. If they enter into agreements with other organisations, including governments, or raise capital from external sources, they do so on terms that ensure democratic control by their members and maintain their cooperative autonomy.

5. Education, Training and Information

Co-operatives provide education and training for their members, elected representatives, managers, and employees so they can contribute effectively to the development of their co-operatives. They inform the general public - particularly young people and opinion leaders - about the nature and benefits of co-operation.

6. Cooperation among Co-operatives

Cooperatives serve their members most effectively and strengthen the cooperative movement by working together through local, national, regional and international structures.

7. Concern for Community

Cooperatives work for the sustainable development of their communities through policies approved by their members.

BIBLIOGRAPHY

Abdullah Öcalan, "Beyond State, Power and Violence"

ANF News, "Efrîn Canton Ministry of Agriculture launches first project" ANF News: "Rapid efforts for agricultural sector in al-Tabqa's"

ANF News, "Al-Tabqa: Massive forestation campaign to be launched by 2018"

ANF News, "Li Cizîrê projeya parzgeha xwezayî"

Anja Flach, Ercan Ayboga, Michael Knapp, "Revolution in Rojava"

Executive Summary (UNEP – WHO), "Guidelines for the Safe Use of Excreta and Wastewater in Agriculture and Aquaculture"

Friedrich Engels, "Dialectics of Nature"

Friedrich Engels, "The Origin of the Family, Private Property and the State"

International Centre for Agricultural Research in the Dry Areas (ICARDA), "The Challenges of Wastewater Irrigation in Developing Countries"

Murray Bookchin, "The Ecology of Freedom: The Emergence and Dissolution of Hierarchy"

Murray Bookchin, "Remaking Society"

Pieter Both & Wim Zwijnenburg, "Syria – the toxic footprint of war"

Rêveberiya parêzgehan a Kantona Cizîrê, "Ji bo parastina parêzgehan biryarên girîng"

Silvia Federici, "Caliban and the Witch"

Sustainable Development Mechanisms Programme, UNFCCC Secretariat, "Afforestation, Reforestation and Forest Restoration in Arid and Semi-arid Tropics"

Swedish Institute for Infectious Disease Control, "Guidelines on the Safe Use of Urine and Faeces in Ecological Sanitation Systems"

Swiss Federal Institute of Technology, "Grey-water treatment on household level in developing countries"

The Rodale Book of Composting University Press of Florida, "Sustainable Urban Agriculture in Cuba"

BIBLIOGRAPHY

CONTACT AND DONATE

Make Rojava Green Again

contact@makerojavagreenagain.org
www.makerojavagreenagain.org
facebook.com/GreenRojava
twitter.com/GreenRojava

Internationalist Commune

contact@internationalistcommune.com
www.internationalistcommune.com
facebook.com/CommuneInt
twitter.com/CommuneInt

Donations to:

Beneficiary: Xarxa Autogestió Social SCCL
IBAN: ES43 1491 0001 2420 8685 5729
BIC/SWIFT: TRIOESMMXXX
Bank: Triodos Bank (Spain)
Reference: deposit P3NIA

DOG SECTION PRESS